AF585212

THE VERY CLEVER
BEE

FELICITY MARSHALL

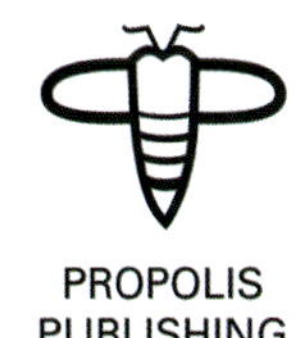

PROPOLIS
PUBLISHING

First published by Propolis Publishing, PO Box 527, Aireys Inlet, Victoria 3231, Australia, 2021
www.propolispublishing.com
Text and illustrations copyright © Felicity Marshall 2021
www.felicitymarshall.com

The moral right of the author has been asserted.
All rights reserved. Without limiting the rights under copyright reserved above, no part of this publication may be reproduced, stored in or introduced into a retrieval system, or transmitted in any form or by any means (electronic, mechanical, photocopying, recording or otherwise) without the prior written permission of both the copyright owner and the above publisher of this book.

Book design by Leo Baker
Prepress by Anne-Marie Reeves
Colour separation by Splitting Image Colour Studios, Clayton, Victoria.
Edited by Helen Chamberlin

Cataloguing in Publication data is available from the National Library of Australia

Every effort has been made to correctly source and attribute copyright of material and quotes produced in this book. The publisher regrets any errors or omissions. Please send any relevant information to Felicity Marshall.

ISBN Hardcover 978-0-6482533-2-7
ISBN Paperback 978-0-6482533-3-4

Printed by Tingleman
The papers used in this book come from 90% recycled sources.

For Marc Carroll, a very clever beekeeper.

Advice From a Honey Bee

Create a buzz
Sip life's sweet moments
Mind your own beeswax
Work together
Always find your way home
Stick close to your honey
Bee yourself

Ilan Shamir

This pear would not exist without the honey bee.

Life Cycle of a Fruit Tree

'Can we conceive what humanity would be if it did not know the flowers?'
Maurice Maeterlinck

A pear seed sprouts in the soil. A tree grows and sends out branches and leaves.
After a few years the tree produces beautiful flowers.

Bees visit the flowers and pollinate them.
Fruit and leaves start to form as the flowers die off.

The pears grow to full size over a few months and become ripe and sweet. They are eaten by people, birds, insects and animals.

Animals and birds deposit seeds in their droppings, and people discard cores containing seeds on the ground or in compost. The pear seed sprouts in the soil

What Is Pollination?

'Bees do have a smell you know, and if they don't they should, for their feet are dusted with spices from a million flowers.'
Ray Bradbury

Bees need plants for food and the plants need bees to pollinate them.

Pollen is the fine powdery substance found in flowers. Pollination is the process of taking pollen from the male part of the flower to the female part of another flower so that new seeds will form. When this happens, fruits, nuts or vegetables will then grow on the plants.

Static electricity attracts pollen to bees. Bees build up a positive charge on their bodies as they fly. When the bee arrives at a negatively charged flower, sparks don't fly, but pollen does.

There are up to 32 kilograms of pollen in one bee colony.

A honey bee visits 50–100 flowers during a collection trip.

There are about 20,000 bee species worldwide, ranging from fat bumblebees (*Bombus*) to tiny Australian bees only a few millimetres long, and solitary bees that live in the ground. Some of these bees pollinate by buzzing vibration or head banging that causes flowers to release pollen. All bees have long tongues to reach nectar in flowers.

Teddy Bear Bee (buzz pollinator)

Bumble Bee (buzz pollinator)

Blue Banded Bee (head banger)

But by far the most efficient of all pollinators is the honey bee (*Apis mellifera*). This has led to the cultivation of the honey bee over many centuries worldwide, to ensure crop pollination and food supply. No other insect has been so valuable to humankind. Honey bees pollinate more than 65 per cent of our food crops, as well as providing us with sweet honey, wax and propolis.

Anatomy of a Honey Bee

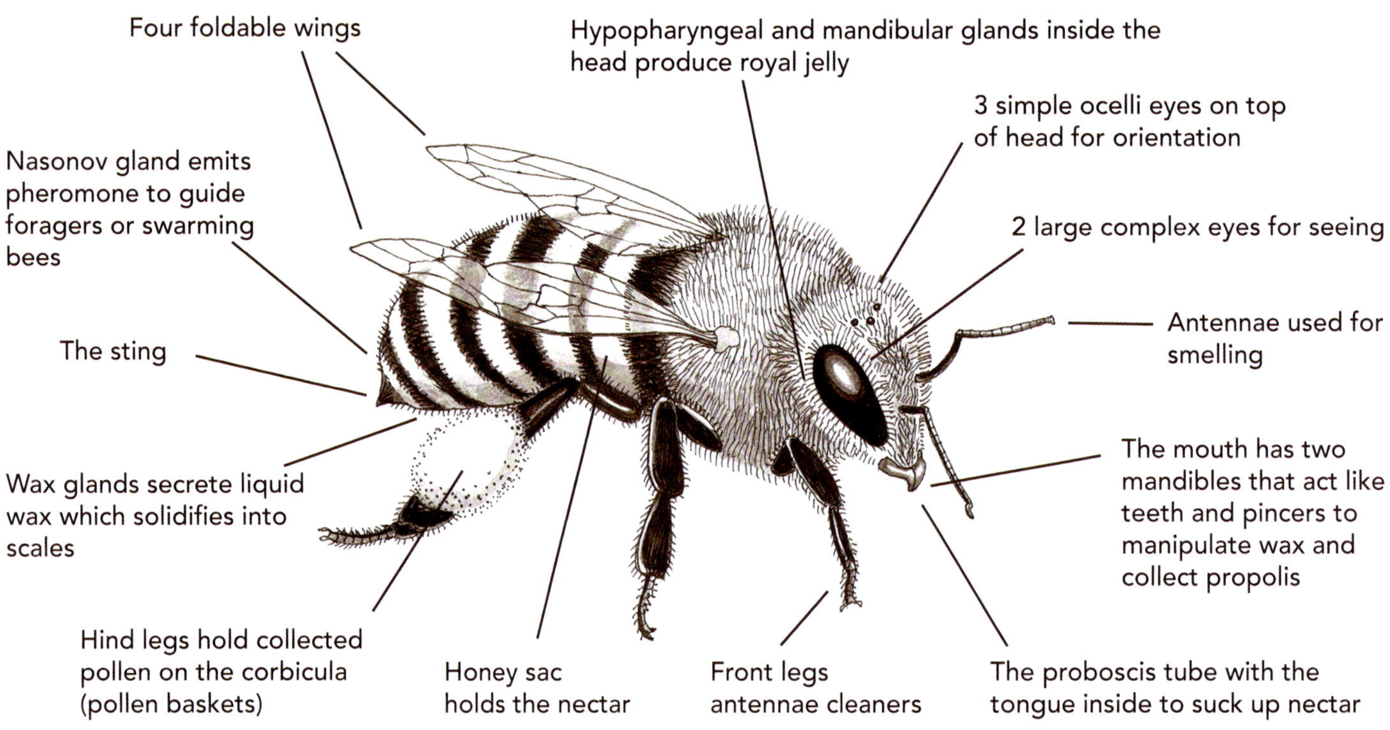

Over millions of years, bees developed hairy bodies, long tongues and other appendages with special adaptations that made them suitable for collecting and carrying nectar and pollen.

Fore, midle and rear legs with pollen baskets

Bee with full pollen baskets on rear legs

Bees quickly learn to recognise colours, fragrances and outlines. This is how they orient themselves in their environment. The portion of the light spectrum that is visible to most insects, including bees, is different from the portion visible to humans. Unlike humans, bees see ultraviolet light as a distinct colour.

'The hum of the bees is the voice of the garden.' ***Elizabeth Lawrence***

Anatomy of a Flower

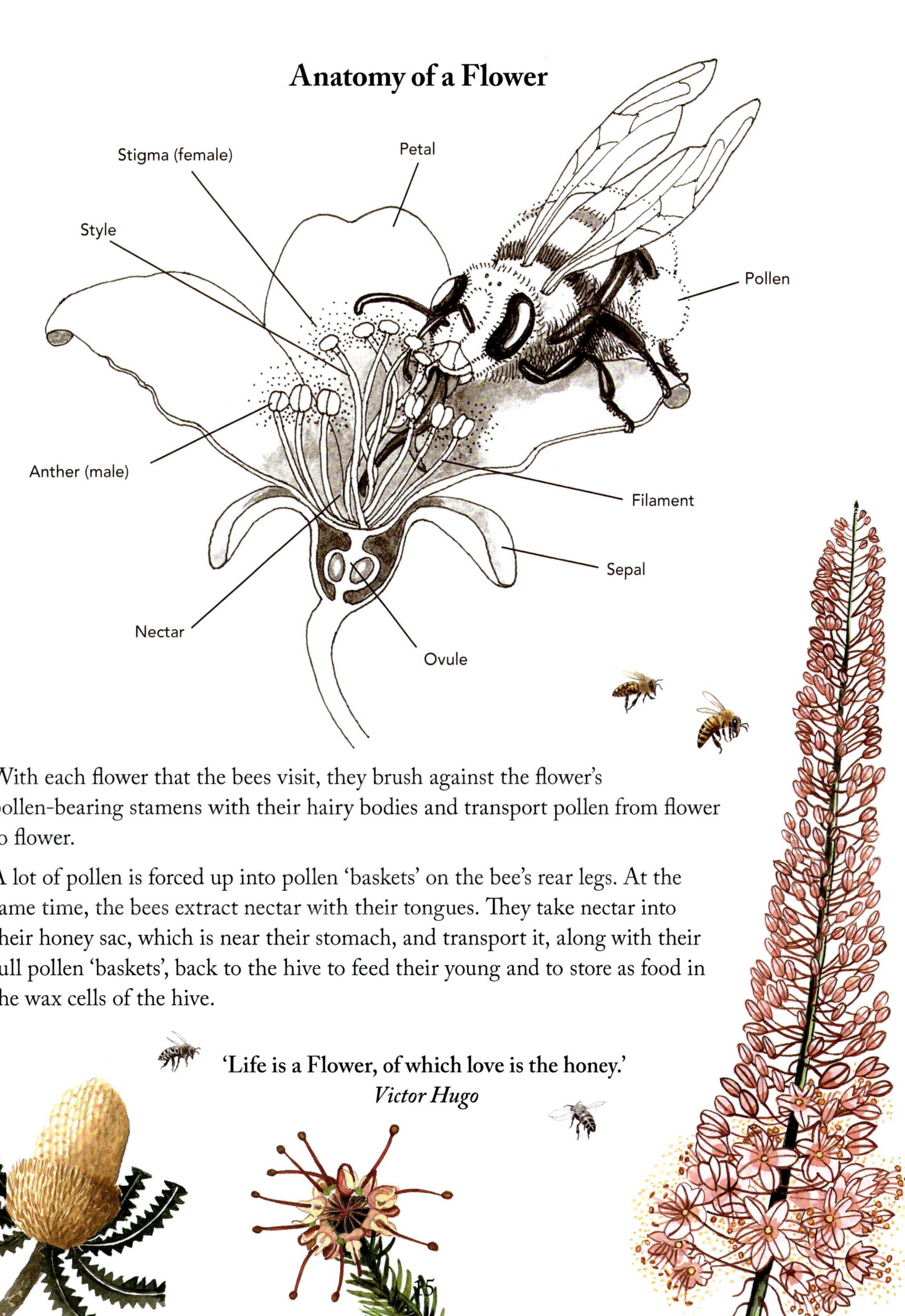

With each flower that the bees visit, they brush against the flower's pollen-bearing stamens with their hairy bodies and transport pollen from flower to flower.

A lot of pollen is forced up into pollen 'baskets' on the bee's rear legs. At the same time, the bees extract nectar with their tongues. They take nectar into their honey sac, which is near their stomach, and transport it, along with their full pollen 'baskets', back to the hive to feed their young and to store as food in the wax cells of the hive.

'Life is a Flower, of which love is the honey.'
Victor Hugo

Life Cycle of a Honey Bee

'The only reason for being a bee that I know of is to make honey. And the only reason for making honey is so I can eat it.' *Winnie The Pooh*

The queen bee lays eggs in the hexagonal cells in the beehive. She lays up to 2000 eggs a day.

They are the size of a very tiny seed.

The eggs hatch into tiny larvae-like caterpillars.

The worker bees feed the larvae as they grow.

The larvae shed their skin several times as they grow larger. After six days they stop eating.

The worker bees now seal the cell using a mixture of wax and propolis.

During the next twelve days each larva in its own cell will spin a cocoon and form legs and wings and turn from a grub (larva) into an insect (pupa).

When this change is complete, she will eat her way through the cell cap and emerge as a young honey bee.

For a worker bee this process takes twenty-one days, and for a drone twenty-four days.

Honeycomb wax cells are six-sided. These hexagons fit together efficiently without any gaps.

Inside the Hive

A queen can live for more than three years. A worker bee lives for only about six weeks. A drone lives until he has a mating flight high up in the sky with a virgin queen and then he dies. The honey bee colony is continually hatching new worker bees to keep the colony flourishing. As soon as a worker dies, another one or two are hatching.

Worker bees also feed the queen larva in her special, larger cell, and she emerges after only sixteen days. A queen is created when the honey bee colony decides it needs a new queen. The queen cell is large and hangs vertically.

Worker bees putting nectar in cells

Queen Bee laying eggs

Worker bees attending the queen bee

Pollen from different flowers

Nectar and honey cells

Larvae at different stages

Queen cells

Capped larvae cells

Drone cells

The worker bees feed the queen larva intensively on protein-rich royal jelly. At day nine the workers cap her cell and leave her to mature into a queen bee. This metamorphosis from larva (grub) into pupa (insect) and then queen bee takes about another week.

'The honey bee colony is a democracy with a queen at its heart.' *Thomas Seeley*

The Co-evolution of Bees and Flowers

'It was the bumblebee and the butterfly that survived. Not the dinosaur.' *Meridel Le Sueur*

Insects of various types, including solitary bees, existed during the time of dinosaurs. Most of them died out during the Ice Age, when most dinosaurs and many plant and flower species also perished. But some survived, and plants survived as seeds.

Early plants reproduced by wind pollination, but this was unreliable, and gradually plants evolved with distinctive flowers and scents to advertise sweet nectar and attract bees and other insects to pollinate them so that they would reproduce more reliably.

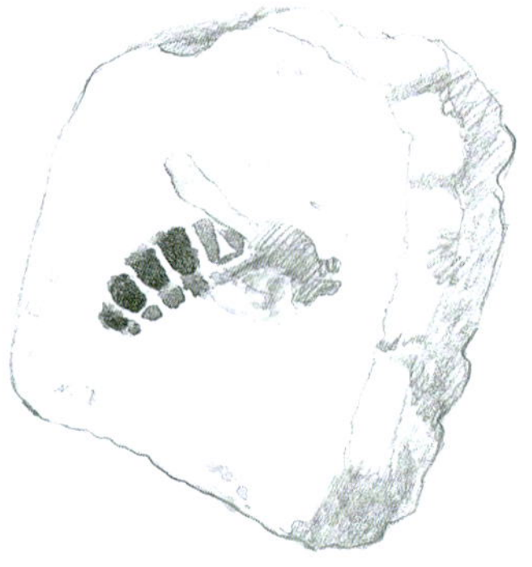

Bee fossil in rock. Approximately 40–65 million years old

Bee fossil in amber Approximately 65 millions years old

A worker bee may visit 2000 flowers per day.

In her lifetime, a worker bee gathers 1/12 of a teaspoon of honey.

From Honey Hunter to Beekeeper

'Honey is the dew distilled from the stars and a rainbow.' *Aristotle*

Rock painting from approximately 15,000 BC

Rock painting from approximately 15,000 BC

Ancient man hunted for honey, finding wild colonies in trees and cliffs. Early Stone Age cave paintings show humans climbing long poles to raid honey stores, which are often very high up on cliffs.

In some parts of the world these methods of honey harvesting are still practised. This is an extremely difficult, dangerous and painful task (causing many stings from angry bees) to reach the sweet prize of honey.

Beekeeping may have occurred by accident thousands of years ago, when swarming wild bees settled in domestic baskets or pots and built their comb inside. This led to people keeping the bees close at hand by building hives for them to live in.

Skep hive

Early beehives woven out of straw are called skeps and they are the classic dome shape often seen in illustrations of beehives.

The skep beehive is a symbol for thrift, industry, orderliness and stability. It is the symbol for the state of Utah in the USA.

Over the centuries, with the development of agriculture and the keeping of animals (rather than just hunting them), beekeeping (apiculture) developed. People discovered the many uses of beeswax and propolis as well as honey. They also discovered the bee's role in pollination. Archaeologists have discovered evidence of hives as early as 8th or 9th century BC in Egypt.

Early beehives were usually round and made of pottery, straw, mud, hollow logs and gourds, but the beekeeper had to break them to harvest the honey. This caused distress to both the bees and the beekeeper.

All over the world there are many different beehives, ranging from simple clay or wooden cylinders to elaborate, highly decorated groups of hives in their own caravan or small cabin.

The Honey Bee Colony

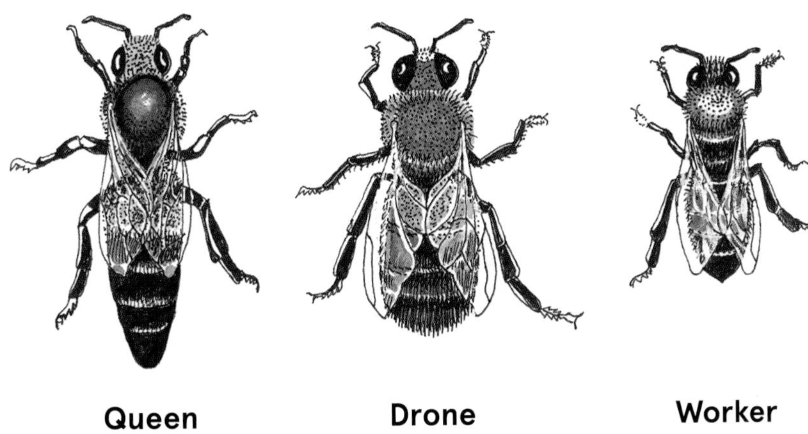

The Queen

Each hive has only one queen. A queen bee is much larger than a worker bee or a drone. Her body is longer, smoother and is not striped. She has a sting, but only uses it to kill another queen. She does not die after stinging, unlike a worker bee. Throughout her egg-laying period the queen emits chemicals or scents called 'pheromones' that reassure and bind the colony together. The queen is completely unable to look after herself and relies on the colony for food, grooming and hygiene.

When she is five to seven days old, a new virgin queen bee leaves on her mating flight. She emits pheromones that attract drones and she mates with several of them, high up in the sky. She returns to the hive and starts to lay eggs. The worker bees will continue to feed and clean her so she can concentrate on egg laying.

The Drones

Drones are male bees. In a hive of 50,000 worker bees, there will be approximately 500 drones. They are larger than worker bees, with big eyes and a blunt body. The cells in which they grow are larger than a worker bee cell. They take twenty-four days from egg to maturity. They do not have a sting, and their sole purpose is to locate a queen and mate with her. After mating a drone will die. When they are not out looking for a queen, they lounge around the hive eating honey and making no contribution to housekeeping! A drone who has not mated and is still in the hive towards the end of summer is no longer welcome and will be kicked out of the hive. With no food or shelter he will soon die.

The honey bee colony is what is known as a 'superorganism' – all members of the colony need each other to survive and thrive. One honey bee on its own will die.

The Workers

Worker bees are all female. They are the bees that we see in our gardens. They have many roles in the hive – cleaners, housekeepers, nurses, queen-attendants, guards, builders, food collectors and undertakers.

When a worker bee hatches from her cell, her first task is to clean her own cell and then clean and prepare cells for the queen to lay her eggs in. A few days later she feeds older larvae with honey and pollen. Then, as she develops further, she secretes royal jelly and feeds this to the younger larvae. Her wax glands develop next, and she caps the larvae cells and the honey cells with wax from her own body.

When she is two weeks old, she takes nectar and pollen from older worker bees returning from foraging. She stores this food in the cells. Then she will start to guard the entrance to the hive. Her sting is fully developed now, and so are her mandibles, which act like teeth in a pincher motion. She will sting any intruder bee or wasp that attempts to enter the hive.

At three weeks, after a few orientation flights, she spends the rest of her short life (about three more weeks at the height of summer) foraging – collecting pollen, nectar, propolis and water. Some worker bees will live through winter, eating honey and rarely going outside the hive. Worker bees' wings wear out from their incessant foraging.

The honey bee colony

'Little bird of Paradise,
She works her work both neat and nice;
She pleases God, she pleases man,
She does the work that no man can.'
Roman bee riddle

What is the difference between a wasp and a bee?

Wasps are predators

- Prey on other insects and are attracted to meat and other food that humans eat.
- Will also eat overripe fruit and nectar
- Hang around barbecues and picnics
- Attracted to lights at night
- Have distinctly black and bright yellow shiny bodies with a narrow waist
- Build nests out of papery cells
- Don't hibernate
- Are aggressive
- Sting repeatedly and will not die. Sting is more painful than a bee sting.

Bees are foragers

- Visit flowers for nectar and pollen, and trees and shrubs for propolis
- Eat only honey
- Have rounded furry bodies with flattened legs for collecting pollen
- Range in colour from black/brown with orange, tan or yellow stripes.
- Build their homes out of wax
- Hibernate in winter and eat stored honey
- Only sting when feeling threatened.
- Die after stinging

Bees in close-up can look like monsters!

Activity in the Bee Colony

'The spirit of the hive – work or die.' *Maurice Maeterlinck*

The beehive in spring and summer is a 'hive of activity'. Bees make a 'bee line' for the best flowers and blossom. If you are in their flight path, they may bump into you! They also collect propolis which comes from the sap and buds of trees and use it as a thin antibacterial and anti-fungal coating on the inside walls of the hive, to strengthen their cells and to fill any cracks. The air is filled with their buzzing and the hive has a beautiful aroma of honey. Bees flying and visiting bright flowers is one of the joys of spring and summer.

Some bees in each hive act as 'heater bees' and raise their body heat several degrees to keep the brood of baby bees at a constant temperature.

Providing Food

Worker bees return from foraging, carrying nectar and pollen which is fed to the growing bee larvae or stored in hexagonal cells. Summer is the busiest time of the year, and bees with legs laden with colourful pollen can be seen returning to the hive. The bees fan their wings to keep the hive at a constant temperature of 35°C (95°F), do the 'waggle dance' to show their sisters where to find the best flowers, guard the entrance or look after the developing baby bees in the brood box.

Nectar To Honey

The process of converting nectar into honey begins in the bee's honey sac (located just above her stomach), where an enzyme called invertase is added to the nectar. The returning forager bees deposit the nectar into the mouths of house bees who then deposit the nectar into the wax cells.

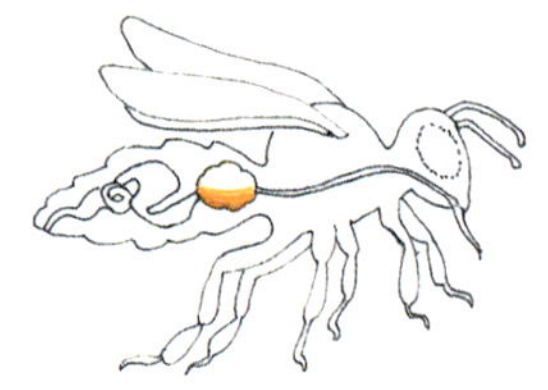

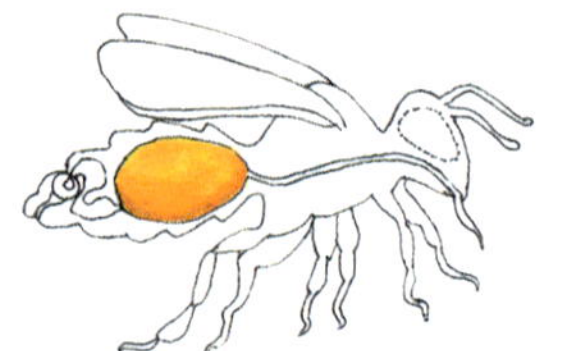

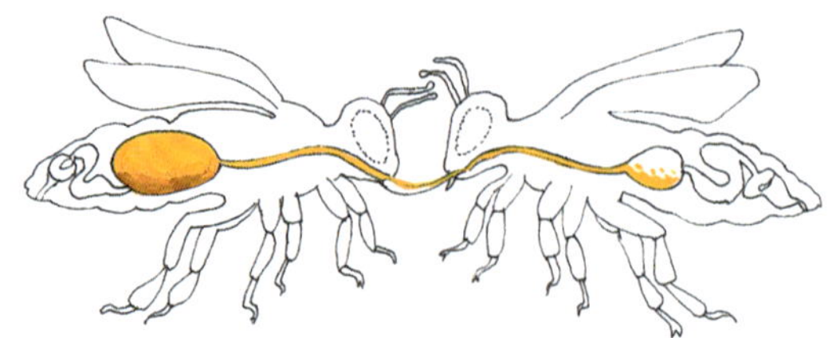

The house bees fan the nectar to reduce the water content to 19 per cent to complete its conversion into honey. The bees now build a wax capping over each cell of honey.

Seasonal Changes

In autumn, as the weather cools, so does the availability of flowers and tree blossom. The bees' activity slows and the beekeeper will now reduce the size of the hive but still leave plenty of honey to provide food for the bees in winter. If it is a harsh winter or spring the bees may run out of stored food. The beekeeper may feed them sugar syrup to keep them alive until they can forage for nectar again.

In spring, when there is a population increase and a hive gets too crowded or the queen is becoming too old or inefficient, her pheromones change, and this is a signal to the colony that they need to create a new queen. The old queen will either leave the hive, taking several drones and half of the workers with her — a process called 'swarming'. Or she will kill the new queen. Or the new queen will kill her. Or one of them will be ejected.

Bee colonies reproduce by swarming. Before swarming, bees gorge themselves on honey, then accompany the queen when she flies out of the hive. They will then create a new colony in a new home – sometimes in a hollow tree, but not always in a location that is suitable to humans! During this time, the bees are docile and easy to manage and can be gently dropped into an empty hive box or cardboard box. Then the beekeeper can install them into a new hive.

Bee Communication

'The honey bee uses the most complex symbolic language of any animal on earth, outside of the primate family.' *Karl Von Frisch*

Buzzing

Bees flap their wings about 230 times a second and that is what creates the buzzing sound. When they are disturbed or threatened, their buzzing becomes louder and more aggressive.

Piping

A young queen pipes to communicate to all the bees in the colony, especially any other queen. She is letting the other queen know of her presence and her willingness to fight to be the only queen in the hive.

Dancing

The returning forager bee performs the 'waggle dance' to inform other bees where sources of nectar are to be found. The dance shows the bees two things – distance and direction. Bees have a solar compass, enabling them to remember where things are in relation to the sun.

At the same time, a bee will give her sister bees some nectar to sample from the particular area. She will also have the flowers' scent on her body.

Austrian zoologist Karl von Frisch spent nearly fifty years observing bee communication. His findings on the bee's waggle dance earned him a Nobel Prize.

The waggle dance

Bees festooning while building wax cells

Posture

Bees' alarm posture (tail in the air) exposes their Nasonov gland to alert other bees to the presence of a predator or danger. A different posture welcomes foragers back to the hive.

Pheromones

Bees emit different pheromones (scents) for different reasons – to mate, to guide nectar-foragers home, to warn of attack. When a worker bee stings, she releases the 'sting pheromone' to warn other bees of an enemy.

Vibrating

Bees huddle together and vibrate their bodies to create warmth in winter to keep the hive at 35°C (95°F). They will die if they become too cold.

The Sting

Only female worker bees sting and they will die after stinging. The queen can also sting, but only to kill other queens. She does not die afterwards. Drones do not have a sting.

If you are stung by a bee, pull the sting out of your skin as soon as possible to minimise the amount of venom. The sting looks like a very tiny thorn and may be quickly scraped out with a fingernail or pulled out with tweezers.

It is normal for most people to get a localised reaction from a sting – soreness, a little swelling. This settles down after a while and a day or so later the sting site may become itchy.

Occasionally some people have an allergic reaction known as anaphylaxis. This may lead to a hospital visit. Wasp stings have the same effect.

'Float like a butterfly, sting like a bee.' *Mohammed Ali*

The Structure of a Modern Hive

'No work, no money. No bees, no honey.' *Proverb*

The modern hive has a brood box for the queen and her brood of hatching eggs and nurse bees (the 'nursery'), and separate boxes called supers for honey storage (the 'pantry'), that are placed above the brood box.

Each hive box has eight to ten removable frames inside that have wax sheets attached. Bees work on several sheets of wax comb at a time, building up wax cells. The space between each frame is small enough to keep the hive snug and for the bees to remain in close contact with each other while still being able to move around in the darkness of the hive. If the gap was any bigger the bees would fill it up with propolis or wax! This keeps the hive at a constant temperature and ensures a snug home for the bees.

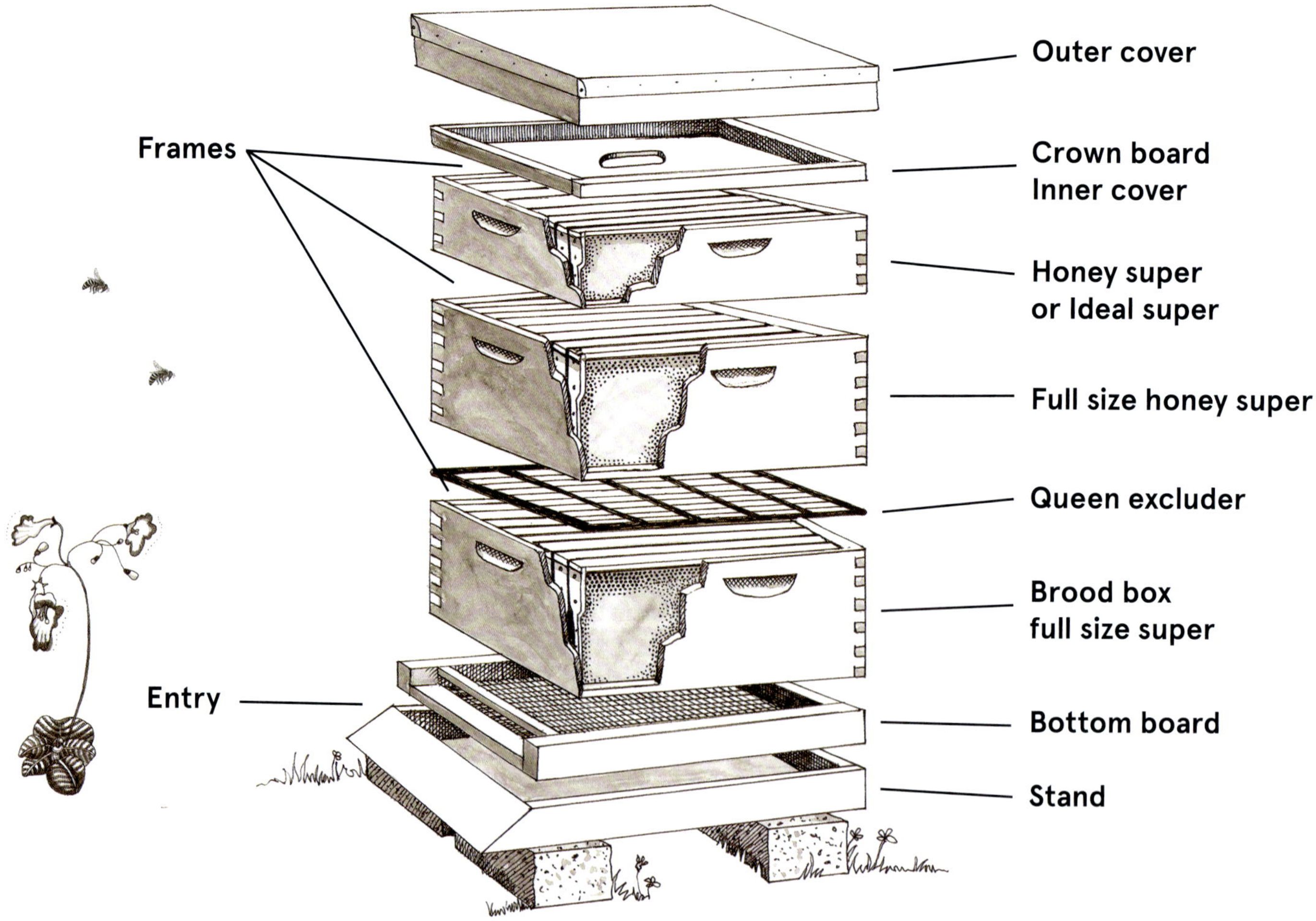

Outer cover
Frames
Crown board
Inner cover
Honey super
or Ideal super
Full size honey super
Queen excluder
Brood box
full size super
Entry
Bottom board
Stand

Typical Langstroth beehive

As the bee population quickly grows in the brood box, it becomes necessary to add a super on top. As the colony continues to grow and needs more space the beekeeper will add more supers to the hive and the bees will fill these with honey.

With care, these hives can be regularly checked for disease or other problems without damaging the physical well-being and harmony of the colony.

'No living creature, not even man, has achieved in the centre of his sphere, what the bee has achieved,' *Maurice Maeterlinck*

Discoveries and Innovations in Beekeeping

A turning point in beekeeping occurred when American Reverend Langstroth patented the 'removable frame' hive in the mid-19th century and it is now used worldwide. This system is the most efficient and kind way to keep bees as hives no longer have to be destroyed to obtain honey.

The Flow Hive

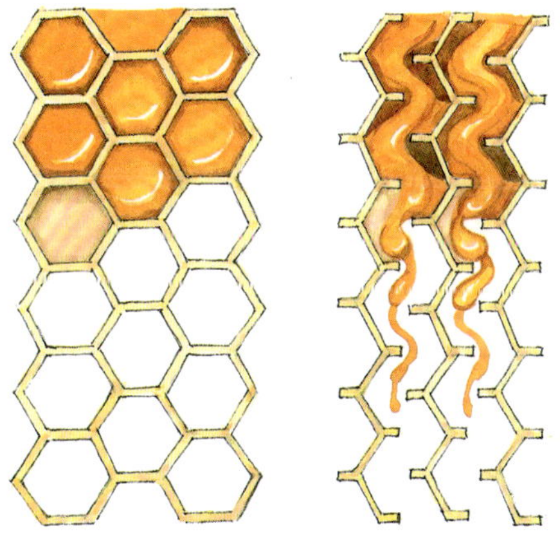

The split cell system

In 2015 Australians Stuart and Cedar Anderson invented The Flow Hive. The first automatic honey-harvesting device in history, the system works by splitting the cells into an offset position. The honey runs out of the cells and into a tube that takes it outside the hive and into jars. The cells are closed again and the bees repair and restore the broken wax. However, the beekeeper still needs to maintain regular inspection and maintenance of the total hive.

The Beekeeper's Work

Apart from caring for the welfare of the bees, the beekeeper's main task is extracting honey, wax and propolis from the frames. The wax cappings are cut off the filled honey cells. This is done with a special heated knife or with a capping scratcher. The wax cappings fall into a container and will later be melted down into blocks of wax. Propolis is always in tiny amounts and this is scraped off the frames and collected in a separate container. Once the frames are uncapped, they are put into an extractor or spinner. This can be manually operated with a handle, or for bigger commercial honey producers, an electric centrifuge is used. The honey is flung out by centrifugal force. It runs down the side of the extractor and collects in the bottom where it flows out of a tap and through fine mesh strainers into large containers. It is then put into jars and labelled, ready to sell.

Commercial honey producers often heat honey to prevent it crystallising, but this can destroy many of the micro-nutrients and antibacterial properties in the honey. Untreated honey is the most beneficial for your health.

The bees' attack scent is very similar to the smell of bananas. Do not eat a banana before approaching a beehive!

The Modern Beekeeper (Apiarist)

A good beekeeper treats the bees with respect and care. He/she is quiet and gentle while handling the hive. This ensures that the bees do not get upset and that they don't fear the beekeeper. The optimum time to inspect a beehive is on a still, warm day between the hours of 10 am and 3 pm when the worker bees are out foraging.

The beekeeper wears a protective suit which is either white or a light colour. It has elastic around ankles and wrists so that bees can't get inside. It has a built-in hood and veil, or else the beekeeper wears a hat with a veil, as well as long leather gloves and boots.

Some Beekeeping Tools

The smoker is used to calm the bees. Pine needles, cardboard, bark or dry leaves are used as fuel.

The hive tool, which is used to lever open the boxes and lift out frames.

The bee brush, which is used to gently brush bees off frames.

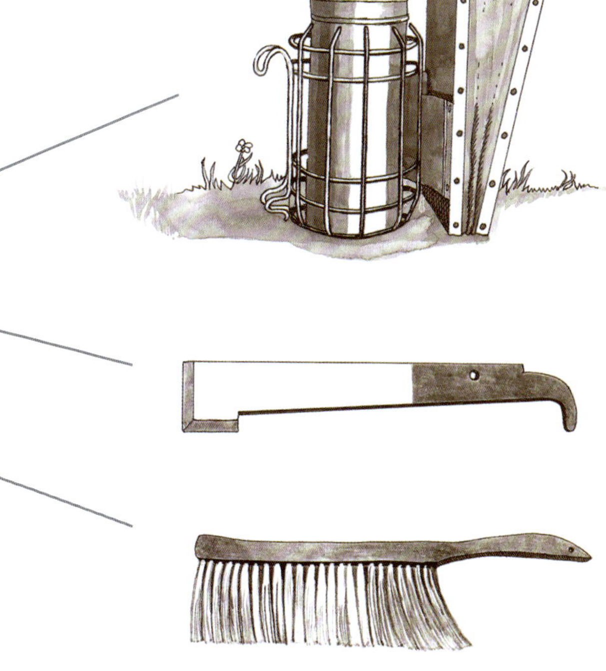

Honey

Honey is used in cookery and confectionary. For thousands of years it was the only sweetener known, until the discovery of sugar. Mead is an alcoholic drink made from honey.

Honey is a superb preservative; it is hygroscopic, (absorbs water) and antimicrobial, so when it comes into contact with animal tissue, it slowly releases hydrogen peroxide, which in turn slowly inhibits bacterial growth.

There are many medical and pharmaceutical uses for honey. Apitherapy is the name given to therapies made from honey. Manuka honey from New Zealand and some Australian honeys have exceptional antibacterial healing properties and have been used on burns, ulcers and wounds.

Natural honey is also used in cough and cold remedies and for hayfever relief.

A superior ingredient in beauty products such as moisturisers, cleansers and shampoos, honey has been known for thousands of years to be beneficial to the skin and was used by great beauties throughout history and up to the present day. It is often combined with beeswax and flower scents or oils.

I eat my peas with honey,
I've done it all my life.
It makes the peas taste funny,
But it keeps them on the knife!
Ogden Nash

Cleopatra famously bathed in a mixture of honey and milk.

Embalming with honey dates back to the 2nd century BC. Bodies were smeared with beeswax and immersed in honey. The ancient Egyptian Pharaohs were embalmed in such a way.

Beeswax

Beeswax is produced from the bee's body and then chewed to soften it before use. It has many uses, the most well-known being candle-making. The church used beeswax candles for centuries because of its purity and sweet fragrance.

Bee producing wax scales

Chewing wax to soften it

- Sealing wax was a foolproof way of sealing documents
- Furniture polish is made from a blend of beeswax, oils and pure turpentine
- A vital ingredient in cosmetics and make-up
- Artists' paints and mediums
- A lubricant on drawers, zippers and skis to reduce friction, on needles for seamstresses and on nails or screws for carpenters
- Surfers wax their boards to increase grip as do archers on their bow strings
- Men use wax to hold their moustache shape, and to create dreadlocks
- Sculptors and jewellers use beeswax to create fine, detailed designs
- Batik fabric and Easter eggs have wax designs on them before being dyed
- Cheesemakers coat their cheeses with wax as a natural protection
- Beeswax is used for polishing and softening leather
- Gardeners use beeswax to seal grafts
- Musicians use beeswax in didgeridoos, accordions and violins

Propolis

Propolis is combined with beeswax and other ingredients to make a fine wood varnish, notably used by Stradivarius, the famous violin maker. It is used in natural therapies and herbal medicines, usually combined with pollen and other ingredients. It is also made into an ointment for rashes and abrasions. Propolis is used in cosmetics, lipsticks, toothpaste, shampoo and soap. Pollen, bee venom and royal jelly are also used in some cosmetics and natural remedies.

Q: How many everyday things can you find in the illustration on the next page that make use of honey, beeswax or propolis?' *Answers page 46.*

CLEOPATR
S BATH
FLOUR
CREMA

SAINT AMBROSE
WAX

Hazards, Disease and Predators

'The greatest enemy to the honey bee is mankind itself.'
William Longgood

There is a decline in honeybee populations globally and this is due to several factors:

Hazards

Herbicides, pesticides and other chemicals sprayed on crops cause illness, sterility, paralysis and death to millions of bees worldwide.

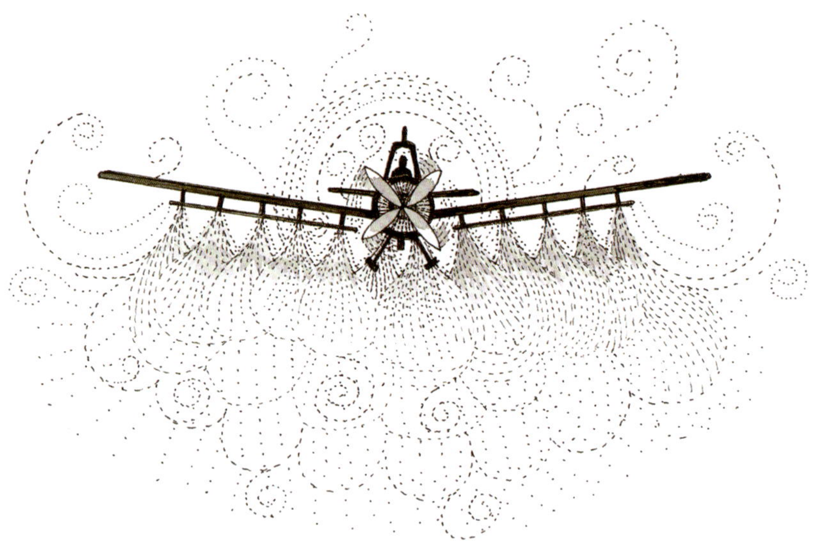

Bees and all other insects were wiped out in a bout of crop spraying using chemical pesticides in one region in China. Subsequently, teams of labourers had to hand pollinate all their fruit trees and plant crops by hand, using special paint brushes. They were nowhere near as efficient as bees.

Industrialised Beekeeping

In some countries, tens of millions of bees are trucked each spring to pollinate vast monocultures of almonds, blueberries and other crops. Millions of bees usually die after the pollination period. Even for surviving bees, disease often follows the distress of homelessness, disorientation, and being unable to follow natural behaviours.

Diseases

Like all living creatures, bees are vulnerable to various diseases and parasites. Neglect by the beekeeper allows disease to take hold.

Predators

Bears have for millions of years been the honey bees' biggest predator, breaking open hives and feasting on honey and bee larvae. Raccoons and badgers will also raid hives. Birds such as woodpeckers, bee-eaters, swallows, thrushes and magpies will also eat bees. Mice and rats will attempt to enter the hive to feast on honey and larvae. Wasps and robber bees in search of honey are a constant threat.

Climate Change and Forest Clearing

Erratic flowering by many plants due to climate change, and the loss of flowering forests and wilderness due to land clearing for development have contributed to the decline in honey bee populations. If the honey bee continues to decline, scientists claim that they will disappear permanently from our world, along with much of its beauty, food and fragrance.

How Bees Help Humans

'Bees are 'humanity's greatest friend among the insects.'
Michael Schacker

Honey bees have existed for 60 to 80 million years compared to humans, who are about three million years old. Bees are the earth's supreme pollinators, providing us with food by pollinating flowers to ensure that they reproduce in the form of fruit, vegetables, seeds and nuts. They also pollinate fibre crops, cotton, flax (linen) and hemp, from which we make clothing. Pollination also guarantees that flowers will continue to grow on planet earth and that pasture crops for animals will flourish.

The honey bees' pollination services to the world are worth many billions of dollars in terms of agriculture and trade. Flowers are used in medicines, pharmaceuticals, cosmetics, perfume-making and as a cookery ingredient, as well as delighting us with their beauty and fragrance. The flowers and leaves of plants have been used to heal, boost immunity, beautify and calm human beings for centuries.

Recognising their extraordinary sense of smell, researchers have successfully trained honey bees to detect drugs, explosives and other illegal substances in clinical trials. They claim that honey bees could eventually replace sniffer dogs at airports. The honey bee can be trained in ten minutes to stick out its tongue when it smells a particular substance. A dog needs at least three months' training to achieve the same result. Bees' phenomenal sense of smell is also being used to trial their ability to detect certain cancers in medical tests.

'Vote #1 Bees
– they know what they are doing.'
Michael Leunig

Keeping Bees and Ourselves Safe and Happy

Bees are wild creatures and need to be treated with respect. Like all wild creatures, if you come close to their home (hive) with young inside, they will chase you away, possibly sting you. So, keep your distance. Keep away from the hive entrance and the bees' flight path. Because they may accidentally fly into you as they make a 'bee line' to some flowers – you may wrongly think you are being attacked. And bees often mistake dogs for bears, so keep your pets away from hives.

The beekeeper is dressed in protective clothing and knows how and when to handle the bees safely and calmly. A good beekeeper wants to have happy, healthy bees. It is a mutually beneficial relationship.

Bees will forage in a radius of up to 5km (3 miles).
But it is more efficient to have the nectar source close by.

How We Can Help Bees

To help bees we should:

- Reduce the clearing of forests and wilderness.
- Fill our gardens, no matter how small, with trees, shrubs and plants that will flower to provide nectar for bees.
- If you have a vegetable garden, let your parsley, lettuce, carrots and broccoli go to flower in autumn. Bees love the pollen and nectar on these blossoms. And you can gather seeds for next year!
- Don't spray pesticides or weed killers on your garden. They will kill lots of beneficial insects, like ladybirds, hoverflies, moths and butterflies as well as bees.
- Use organic gardening practices – natural bug and weed management, organic fertilisers, compost and mulch.
- Buy natural honey from your local beekeepers wherever possible. They are committed to the welfare of bees, and to producing fine honey.
- If you come across a swarm of bees, don't be afraid and certainly don't try to kill them. Call a swarm-collection service in your area, as they know how to carefully catch the swarm and find a new safe home for the bees.
- If you see bees in your garden – watch, don't touch. They are tiny wild animals.
- Remember we are all part of the earth's ecosystem – earth, oceans, fish, plants, insects, animals and humans.

'If we die, we are taking you with us.' *The Bees*

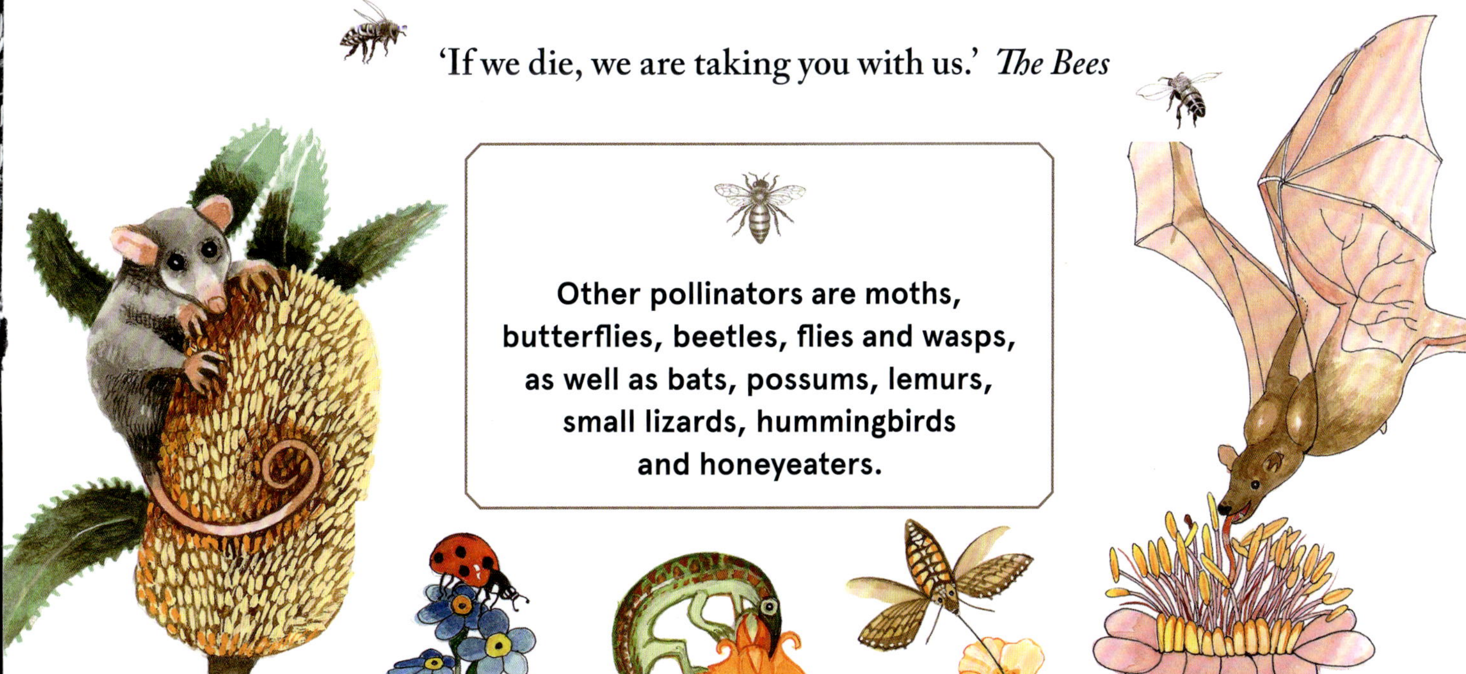

Other pollinators are moths, butterflies, beetles, flies and wasps, as well as bats, possums, lemurs, small lizards, hummingbirds and honeyeaters.

Answers to use of honey, beeswax and propolis

1. Honey is used in cookery and confectionary. Mead is a honey drink.
2. Medical uses for honey to heal burns, ulcers and wounds.
3. Gardeners use honey on plant cuttings and beeswax on grafts.
4. Cleopatra bathed in a mixture of honey and milk.
5. Honey and beeswax are used in cosmetics and beauty products.
6. Beeswax candles
7. Beeswax is used in furniture and leather polish.
8. Archers use wax on their bow strings.
9. Artists' paints and mediums.
10. Surfer's board wax.
11. Beeswax to hold moustaches, and to create dreadlocks.
12. Sculptors and jewellers use beeswax to create designs.
13. Batik fabric design.
14. Decorated Easter eggs.
15. Cheesemakers coat their cheeses with wax
16. Musicians use beeswax in didgeridoos and accordions.
17. Propolis and beeswax make a fine wood varnish for musical instruments.
18. Propolis is used in skin ointment, toothpaste, soap and shampoo.
19. Sealing wax on letters and documents.

'We have rather chosen to fill our lives with honey and wax; thus furnishing mankind with the two noblest of things, which are sweetness and light.'

Jonathan Swift